W9-AMZ-605

World's Fastest Machines

BULLET TRAINS

Charles Hofer

PowerKiDS press

New York

Published in 2008 by The Rosen Publishing Group, Inc.
29 East 21st Street, New York, NY 10010

First Edition

Editor: Jennifer Way
Book Design: Greg Tucker
Photo Researcher: Nicole Pristash

Photo Credits: Cover © Gavin Hellier/Getty Images; p. 5 Shutterstock.com; p. 7 © Topical Press Agency/Getty Images; p. 9 © Three Lions/Getty Images; p. 11 © age fotostock/SuperStock; p. 13 © Ministry of Land Infrastructure and Transport/Getty Images; p. 15 © Koichi Kamoshida/ Getty Images; p. 17 © Yoshikazu Tsuno/AFP/Getty Images; p. 19 © Denis Charlet/AFP/Getty Images; p. 21 © www.iStockphoto.com/Luke Daniek.

Library of Congress Cataloging-in-Publication Data

Hofer, Charles.
  Bullet trains / Charles Hofer. — 1st ed.
      p. cm. — (World's fastest machines)
  Includes index.
  ISBN 978-1-4042-4174-9 (library binding)
  1. High speed trains—Juvenile literature. I. Title.
  TF1450.H58 2008
  385'.22—dc22
                                          2007025687

Manufactured in the United States of America

Contents

High-Speed Trains

Our world moves quickly. Because of our busy lives, we are always looking for the fastest, safest, and cheapest ways to get around. High-speed trains just may be one of the best ways.

Over 50 years ago, the car pushed the train to the edge of **extinction**. Today, thanks to high-speed trains, getting around by railroad is as common as ever. These machines can travel nearly 200 miles per hour (322 km/h). They can move hundreds of people from city to city. High-speed trains may be the **future** of travel, linking cities and countries like never before.

High-speed trains are used all over the world to get people around quickly.

The History of Trains

Trains first appeared in the early 1800s. They were powered by steam engines that ran on coal. These first trains were slow and let out a lot of thick, black smoke. The steam train allowed people and businesses to move from the United States' East Coast to the Midwest and the West. By 1869, the **transcontinental railroad** was completed and rail lines connected, or linked, the United States' Atlantic coast with its Pacific coast.

Everything changed with the invention of the car in the early 1900s. Cars and roads allowed people more freedom in travel. They no longer needed to live and work near rail lines.

This is a steam-powered train from the early 1900s. Trains like this one helped connect the cities that had spread across the United States.

The Dawn of High-Speed Trains

By the 1940s, the railroad business looked like it was going to fail. Cars had become the most common way for people to get around. Trains needed to change with the times. First, trains went electric in the 1950s. Soon, trains were going well over 100 miles per hour (161 km/h). By the 1960s, high-speed trains led to a new period in travel.

At the 1964 Tokyo Olympics, Japan opened the Shinkansen. It would become known as the bullet train and change **mass transit**. Over the years, the Shinkansen system of rail lines became faster. Today, the Shinkansen 500 line trains can reach speeds of nearly 200 miles per hour (322 km/h)!

Built for Speed

Bullet trains are as cool looking as they are fast. Their new, **aerodynamic design** allows them to cut through the air as they speed down the track.

Nations with high-speed trains try to outdo each other with speed and new designs. Japan's JS500 Shinkansen train looks more like a fighter jet than a train. The AVE Talgo 350, in Spain, is shaped to cut down on noise pollution. Noise pollution is the loud sounds made by machines, which can sometimes be bad for people's ears.

Spanish AVE trains have an aerodynamic design that helps them go fast while making as little noise as possible.

Safety First

High-speed trains not only have to be fast, they also have to be very safe. Japan has led the way in building the fastest trains and the safest trains. This is because the island nation gets **earthquakes** and **typhoons**. The Shinkansen is built so well that not one death has been reported on the train line during its four decades of service.

Even the best-designed trains can **derail** if they take a turn at too high a speed. To keep this from happening, some train tracks make the train tilt, or lean, into a turn. This helps cut down the forces that could derail a train making a sharp turn at a high speed.

It takes a strong earthquake to derail a bullet train, like this one in Nagaoka, Japan. Bullet trains are designed so people on the train will not be badly hurt.

The Tracks

Because they go so fast, high-speed trains need special tracks that are different from other kinds of train tracks. These tracks allow the train to move fast without derailing. The design of high-speed train tracks is always changing.

The future of high-speed trains may lie in maglev, or **magnetic** levitation, transport. Maglev trains use magnetic force to float above the rail! When the magnets on the train and on the track are near each other, they repel, or push away from, each other. This is because the magnets have the same charge. This special track allows maglev trains to reach greater speeds.

In late 2003, the Japanese train JR-Maglev broke the all-time speed record when it reached 361 miles per hour (581 km/h)!

The Shinkansen

The Japanese Shinkansen was the first-ever bullet train line and it quickly set a new standard for mass transit. The trains first appeared in 1964 and ran at speeds nearing 130 miles per hour (210 km/h). At the time, the Shinkansen connected only big cities such as Tokyo and Osaka. However, the new train line was very well liked. In just three years, 100 million people had traveled on the line!

Within decades, the Shinkansen system spread across Japan. Today, the Shinkansen 500 line trains are some of the world's fastest, with top speeds of 186 miles per hour (299 km/h).

The latest Shinkansen is the N700 series, which began running in July 2007. The N700 trains can reach speeds up to 186 miles per hour (299 km/h).

The Eurostar

In 1994, the Channel Tunnel opened. The Chunnel, as it is known, crosses the English Channel and connects England with France and Belgium. The Chunnel's train is called the Eurostar. This high-speed train can go from London, England, to Paris, France, in 2 hours and 35 minutes. In 2003, a Eurostar train set a record by reaching 208 miles per hour (335 km/h).

The Eurostar is an **engineering** feat. The three Eurostar nations each have different railroad systems. This means that they had to change these systems to use the high-speed train system. By working together, these nations made the Eurostar a success.

This Eurostar train runs in northern France. One of the Eurostar's goals is to make travel between England, France, and Belgium greener. High-speed trains use less energy than airplanes.

Changing the Way We Travel

High-speed trains are changing the way we travel. People are looking for another choice besides the car to get around. In April 2007, France presented its newest TGV train. It broke a 17-year-old speed record when it reached 357 miles per hour (575 km/h)!

Many nations are designing their own high-speed rail lines. A few of these countries are Spain, Italy, and Belgium. Soon, all of Europe will be connected by high-speed train systems. In the United States, California is leading the way in high-speed rail lines. The state is planning a high-speed line with trains that will go 200 miles per hour (322 km/h).

Trains to Come

As we move toward a greener world and try to make less pollution, high-speed trains look like a way to go. These trains run on cleaner power and can move hundreds of people at once. The result is less pollution caused by cars on the road.

Once near failing, the future looks bright for trains, thanks to high-speed rail lines. For years, engineers have been trying to build a huge system of trains that can travel up to 200 miles per hour (322 km/h) while carrying people to cities of all sizes. This dream might come true very soon.

Glossary

aerodynamic (er-oh-dy-NA-mik) Made to move through the air easily.

design (dih-ZYN) The plan or the form of something.

earthquakes (URTH-kwayks) Shakings of Earth caused by the movement of large pieces of land called plates that run into each other.

engineering (en-juh-NEER-ing) Planning and building engines, machines, roads, and bridges.

extinction (ek-STINK-shun) The state of no longer existing.

future (FYOO-chur) The time that is coming.

magnetic (mag-NEH-tik) Having to do with the force that pulls certain objects toward one another.

mass transit (MAS TRAN-sit) A system of public ways to travel.

transcontinental railroad (trants-kon-tuh-NEN-tul RAYL-rohd) The train system that crossed the United States in the 1800s.

typhoons (ty-FOONZ) Storms that occur in the West Pacific with strong winds and heavy rains.

Index

C
Chunnel, 18

D
design, 10, 14

E
earthquake(s), 12
Europe, 18, 20
Eurostar, 18

J
Japan, 8, 10, 12, 16

M
maglev train, 14
magnet(s), 14
mass transit, 8, 16

P
pollution, 10, 22

S
Shinkansen, 8, 10,
   12, 16
steam engine(s), 6,
   10

system(s), 16, 18, 20

T
track(s), 10, 12, 14
transcontinental
   railroad, 6
typhoon(s), 12

U
United States, 6, 20

Web Sites

Due to the changing nature of Internet links, PowerKids Press has developed an online list of Web sites related to the subject of this book. This site is updated regularly. Please use this link to access the list: www.powerkidslinks.com/wfm/train/